The Book on How to Sell Online, EBay & Amazon

How To Make A Profit 24/7 Using The PROPEL™ Technique

by

Andrew Whitfield

www.h2so.org

P - product sourcing

R - real opportunities

O - outstanding customer service

P - prioritised solutions

E - exceptional acceleration

L - leveraged income streams

www.TheBookOnHowToSellOnline.com

Copyright © 2014 Andrew Whitfield

All rights reserved

No part of this book may be reproduced in any form or by any electronic or mechanical means including information storage and retrieval systems, without permission in writing from the author. The only exception is by a reviewer, who may quote short excerpts in a published review.

The information presented herein represents the views of the author as of the date of publication. This book is presented for informational purposes only. Due to the rate at which conditions change, the author reserves the right to alter and update his opinions at any time. While every attempt has been made to verify the information in this book, the author does not assume any responsibility for errors, inaccuracies, or omissions.

Foreword:

In this powerful and easy-to-read book, Andrew Whitfield shows you how to make money by selling online. Whether you're starting from scratch with absolutely nothing, you have an existing business that needs to grow, or you have stock that's been sitting on the shelf for years and have not managed to sell it in your local area, Andrew reveals the secrets for turning everyday goods into cash. With the help of this amazing book, now is the time to get online, join the vast global marketplace, and become a wealthier person!

Raymond Aaron

New York Times Bestselling Author

www.millionairebusinessbootcamp.com

Contents

Chapter 1: Grasping the Opportunity to Sell Online 10

    Why I started a £1.6 million turnover business 10

    What's your big WHY for making money online? 13

    You're ready to take hold of this opportunity with both hands 15

    Turn your dissatisfaction into action 15

    You have the vision of what's possible 16

    The first steps required to reach your vision 18

    Resistance to change 20

Chapter 2: The Top Five Ways to Sell Online 23

    It's easy to create your own web shop 23

    Don't want any stock? Become an affiliate 29

    eBay 33

    Amazon 39

Play.com 46

Ebid.net 47

Quicksales.com.au 47

Bonanza.com 47

Gumtree 48

Pinterest 48

Your terms and conditions 48

Chapter 3: Discovering What's Selling and How to Take Advantage 51

Easy ways to find out what's selling now 52

Go for a walk 53

Use the "sell anything" approach 55

Discover your niche 58

Chapter 4: How to Achieve Quick Credibility and Positive Feedback Ratings 60

What your customer is looking for? 60

Take action every time 62

Sell to friends and family 64

Invest in yourself.. 65

Chapter 5: The Five Worst Mistakes and How to Avoid Them 66

1. Not talking to your potential customers 66

2. Over pricing and under delivering 72

3. Poor packaging.. 74

4. Not taking advantage of great photos......................... 76

5. Shaky or unprofessional video 79

Chapter 6: The Shocking Truth Behind Free Shipping 82

Why offer free shipping? 83

How to calculate free shipping 85

Take advantage of free shipping..................................... 86

Chapter 7: How to Find Stock in a Crowded Marketplace .. 88

Do you have an urgent requirement for cash? 88

Sell products from your home or garden shed 90

Expanding your existing retail business 92

Growing your website in different directions 94

Chapter 8: Is Your Web Shop a Needle in the Internet Haystack? 97

What's in a domain name? 98

Have the right keywords 100

How to get it right 105

Analyse your market 107

Ask some questions 109

Chapter 9: What You Know and Love Could Make Money Online 112

What do I know? 113

What have I done in the past that may shape my future? 115

Do I have a passion, and is my passion enough?............ 114

Chapter 10: The Seven Golden Rules to Guarantee Success 117

1. Brilliant customer service 118

2. Over deliver and under promise 120

3. Stay in touch 122

4. Fix the problem – Do not procrastinate 124

5. Make sure you would accept your own customer service 126

6. Manage your feedback website comments 130

7. Honest descriptions and good photographs 128

Bonus Page 132

Chapter 1: Grasping the Opportunity to Sell Online

Why I started a £1.6 million turnover business

I started this business purely by accident and from necessity. It was after a chance conversation with a good friend who was trying to sell his items on eBay. He did not have a great deal of technical knowledge of how eBay and the Internet worked but enough of an understanding to list items, and he had made some sales. I, on the other hand, had never purchased or sold anything on, or even considered using, eBay, Amazon, or any other website platform to buy and sell things. I was starting as a complete beginner.

That was three years ago at the time of this writing, and since then I have managed, along with my partner, to create a turnover the equivalent of in excess of £1.6 million. I had no money to put into the business and no job. I was starting from zero. I needed to put money in my pocket to live – my "WHY" to do this was as big as that, to find something that worked and keep replicating it.

I sold anything and everything I could get my hands on – new, old, used, refurbished; I even bought things off eBay, resold them on eBay, and made a profit. I have also made a number of mistakes, some of which I share with you in this book to ensure that you don't make the same mistakes or you're at least aware of them.

Since then, there have been a lot of changes. I now have a great team of people that look after my customer service and warehouse, and they pick and pack the items ready for collection by the couriers. I now also work with other people wanting to sell online by giving them some coaching on how to do this. We now have a distribution warehouse focused on getting product out to the customer as fast as possible by also giving excellent customer service.

On eBay I have received in excess of 28,696 pieces of positive feedback in that three years. I have top seller and power seller status, and on Amazon we have just as good a level of feedback. We have just started using play.com along with our own stand-alone websites.

The Book on How to Sell Online, EBay & Amazon™

pick-pack-post (28696 ☆)

Positive Feedback (last 12 months): 99.7%
[How is Feedback percentage calculated?]
Member since: 01-Oct-06 in United Kingdom
Registered as a Business Seller

This member is an eBay Top-rated seller
✓ Consistently receives highest buyer ratings
✓ Dispatches items quickly
✓ Has earned a track record of excellent service

- item as described, received promptly, great seller, thanks very much
  Mens Blue Size 11 Aqua Shoes Beach Shoes Water Aqua Socks Aquashoes
- Thank you for letting me swap the board, what a great company..
  30 Skimboard Blue Shark Skim Board Bodyboard Surfboard
- great as described
  Windbreak 30ftx4ft Beach Garden Windbreaks Camping Wind Break 15 pole Extra
- Fabulous ebayer! Quality item, great communication and fast delivery. Perfect.
  Extreme Fishing Catapult Hunting Catapult Sling Shot ı
- Thanks, got them really very quick... :))))
  Tulip Flowers Benaya Art Tiles Contemporary Wall Picture Tile Plaque 12x12
- super, thank you :)
  35" Skimboard Blue Black Skim Board Bodyboard Surfboard
- Fast service first class seller AAAAA*****
  French Wine Glass Benaya Art Tiles Contemporary Wall Picture Tile Plaque 11x14
- Excellent service, thank you.
  12 x Assorted 3ft Scarecrow Garden Lawn Allotment Bird Pest Control Scare Crow
- great thank u very much
  Wooden Wall Clock Hand Cut Shaped Novelty Funky Clocks Gift Irish Scooter ms 17
- Fast delivery thanks
  Bestway Outdoorsman 300 Inflatable Dinghy Boat 90" x 48" Swimming Pool 2/3 Man

Therefore, my reader, if I can do it, then I definitely know you can do it, whether you're starting from scratch with absolutely nothing, you have an existing business that needs to grow, or you have even bought stock that's been sitting on the shelf for years and have not managed to sell it in your local area. The time is now right for you to get online, increase your presence, and become a wealthier person – both financially and maybe mentally – with the help of my book.

What's your big WHY for making money online?

So let's have a look where you are now. Do you have access to a computer? Do you have access to the Internet? Do you have access to a camera? If the answer to any one of these is "no," please reread the three questions and think a little deeper about whom you know who has access to the above. Most mobile phones have a camera, most towns have a library or an Internet cafe, and you may even be lucky and have a local council that has a get online scheme that you can join free.

So you see you do not need to have everything in your own house; you just need to have access to them, and to have access you just need to look or ask friends, family, or your local authority. What I would say straightaway is work out what you require from what you're about to do. Are you just looking for a little bit of extra income to help out, or do you have a certain goal in mind? Maybe you want to travel the world, take a holiday, buy a new car, buy a computer, or buy that dress or suit so that you can go out into the big wide world and start to make a name for yourself with a business.

You need to decide what your big "WHY" is. It must be big enough to allow you to focus and stay focused so that you can achieve your goal. If it's too small, woolly, feeble, or just not big enough, it will be hard to achieve because you will stay in your comfort zone. You need to move out of your comfort so ever so slightly and stay out there until it becomes part of your new zone.

You're ready to take hold of this opportunity with both hands

By reading this far, dear reader, you're ready to take hold of the opportunity and seize it with both hands. It will not happen overnight. Everything you do needs some work and some effort on your part. To get to the level I am has taken a lot of work and a lot of effort on both my part and of those around me. So let's get on with moving things forward so that you can see how you can make money selling online.

Turn your dissatisfaction into action

Once you have created your first item for sale and decided which route to market you're going to take – this we will discuss in more detail in Chapter 2 – you just need to follow a few simple steps to get your first new sale. Once you have your first new sale you'll feel elated and then you'll start to look at the numbers. Sale number two will feel equally as good as sale number one, and once you have sale number three you'll then be focusing on getting to sale number 10, then number 20, then number 50, and what a feeling when you get number 100. I still feel elated with the new web shops when they reach these numbers.

There is nothing more beneficial than receiving the praise and great comments from customers' feedback. I have a rule that all my team work to and that is "We are only as good as our last piece of customer feedback." There is another famous rule:

"Rule number one: The customer is always right,

Rule number two: If ever the customer is wrong, reread rule number one."

You have the vision of what's possible

Now you have the vision and the focus you know what's possible, we need to make it happen. Please do not rush out and spend your hard earned money on lots of new stock until we have gone further through the book. Or if you already have the stock and want to get it online, let's just keep hold of the vision for the moment so that it can be done correctly and in a way that it will benefit you greatly by increasing your income.

Firstly, who do you know who you can share your vision with and who will work with you to help you get your vision? Do not work alone. Share what you're doing with somebody else, and make sure that that person is positive and will give you support and help whenever you require it. Before you start it may be worth looking at your local chamber of commerce to see if they've got any events on that you could go and get inspired from other people in business. You may even be surprised to find that there is financial and practical free help and assistance available through your local chamber of commerce.

There are also in every town a number of small business clubs. They're all there to help you network and find new opportunities to sell the product or services. You may have something in your idea that you can offer to that person or business in a way that you can both be rewarded. By going to these events you will be meeting positive like-minded people who will have no problem in parting with helpful hints and tips and advice.

The first steps required to reach your vision

It's advisable to decide what the first steps are when you are moving towards your vision or goal. And one way to look at this is to break it down in the following manner: Draw a horizontal line across a piece of paper with one end "1" and the other end is "10." Let us assume that 1 is where we are now and 10 is your vision.

What you now need to do is break the line down into small chunks and make these chunks so small that they might only be tiny little steps that will start you moving forward. So below I have created a small sample idea for you to take forward.

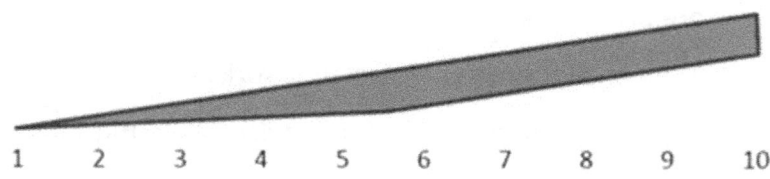

Step number 1: Open an eBay, Amazon, and/or PayPal account.

Step number 2: Spend 30 minutes familiarising yourself with the basic layout of the websites.

Step number 3: Talk to friends, colleagues, acquaintances, or business people on how they have used online shopping facilities.

Step number 4: Make an inventory of the 80% of items you own that you no longer need or require and can sell to make money. If you're an existing business have a look at your stock inventory and find the oldest items that have been sitting on the shelf for the longest period of time without selling.

Step number 5: Search around the Internet to see if anyone else has those items for sale and note down what price they are trying to get for them.

Step number 6: Take a photograph of the item/s from several different angles and decide which one/s other most suitable to give it its best look online.

Step number 7: Write a description of each item. If you're new to doing this, then it may help to speak description into a recording device and play it back as you may find your spoken word is more descriptive.

Step number 8: Find out what keywords (we will cover the keywords in more detail later in the book) people will use to search to find each item where you have listed it.

Step number 9: List your items using all of the previous steps on your chosen selling platform using the appropriate keywords as mentioned above.

Step number 10: Celebrate your success at getting this far.

You may find that you may need to break the steps down even further. This may mean that between steps four and five that you have to make 4a, 4b, 4c, 4d, and so on – you get the idea. Very small steps lead to larger steps, so it's always useful to plan your very small steps first.

Resistance to change

Whenever you start to focus on a new project you may have in the back of your mind, or in some cases the back of other people's minds, a resistance to the change; however, since you have got this far then you have overcome the initial resistance.

This Change Model Formula was created by Richard Beckhard and David Gleicher and is sometimes called Gleicher's Formula:

$$\Delta = D \times V \times F > R$$

Change = Dissatisfaction x Vision x First Steps > Resistance to Change

It's important to note that the three components must all be present to overcome the resistance to change:

1. Dissatisfaction with the present situation,

2. A vision of what's possible in the future,

3. Achievable first steps towards reaching this vision.

If any of the three is zero or near zero, the result will also be zero or near zero and the resistance to change will dominate. If you want to know more, just type in the details above into Google and you will be presented with masses of information on Gleicher's Formula. If you want to get more serious there are many books available and you can source them through detailed searches within Amazon and audio programs available through sites such as audible.com, which is one of my favourites as I can listen to these at my leisure or on a long drive.

Chapter 2: The Top Five Ways to Sell Online

It's easy to create your own web shop

Assuming that you have some knowledge of how the Internet works and perhaps a little experience of working with websites, this could be relatively easy for you. There are a number of packages for sale online at various monthly or annual rates. At this point I would suggest you take some first steps by assessing how competent you are with your knowledge.

Here are a few things that you need to do to get your new shop up and running:

Register a domain name. You need a descriptive domain name that contains a number of keywords to the items, products or service you are offering to your customer.

Host. Before you register your domain name you also need to decide where you're going to host the website. There are a number of opportunities for you to host websites inexpensively. My personal favourite at the time of writing is www.hostgator.com, as they have a package that offers very good value to the types of websites I use.

Build. To build my websites I use something called WordPress, which used to be classed as a free blogging software that you can add numerous plug-ins (some which are free, some chargeable), so that you can get your website more visible, tailored and personalised to your requirements. Google also likes WordPress websites and ranks them quite well in the current search algorithms.

Domain names can normally be purchased on a annual rental basis relatively inexpensively and it's advisable for you to decide whether you require .com, .co, .uk, .eu, etc., and ensure you get the one that's more relevant to which country you are going to trade as this will help you direct traffic to your website.

Domain name keywords. Then when you have researched your keywords, try to make your domain name keyword rich. As an example, if I were selling motorbike spares in Croydon, I would want to get a website domain name registered something like croydonmotorbikespares.co.uk. More on the very names in chapter 8.

Merchant account. To enable me to take credit card payments I would need to open a merchant account. This can be done with your local bank if you have an existing business bank account, or you can search merchant services in Google and research the comparisons on their charges, which tend to vary quite a lot; and you also need to consider how quickly they will transfer the money into your bank account.

When looking at merchant services they may also require information about the product or service that you're selling including guarantee periods, money-back or refund terms, and conditions. One point to remember when discussing this is that if you're offering long-term 100% money-back guarantee periods they may decide to retain a hold on a sum of money until that period expires or until you have built up enough credibility with your service provider. This could have a major impact on your cash flow so always be aware and ask the question to see if they are going retain a hold on your money for a period of time.

PayPal is one of the most recognised and universal ways of being paid by customers and is becoming ever more popular. They also have the ability to accept credit and debit cards on your behalf, and they have pricing plans to suit the volume of business that you will transact. Just go to PayPal.com and search for merchant services for more information.

With PayPal you will also have the ability to accept instant payment from the customer's PayPal account, which is normally preloaded with available funds. They have new ways of you accessing your money fairly quickly and that even includes a PayPal debit card which can be used under the MasterCard brand so that you can access your money whenever and wherever you require it.

I also allow direct transfer of money into my bank account, where if the customer requests it they will get the IBAN or BIC number, account number, sort code which will allow them to deposit money directly and in most cases instantaneously.

Photos. Obtain a decent camera for taking photographs and also consider using lights, light boxes and possibly backdrops to ensure your product will stand out. It's advisable to take crisp and clear pictures on a plain background, preferably white, to show the product at its best. Always remember the person is purchasing the picture before they are purchasing your written description.

Video. You should also be able to use video techniques to enhance your website, and there are lots of clever tools that you can use to create inexpensive video whether you're using a number of still pictures, being interviewed, or showing your product in 360° detail.

Pay-per-click. Decide on any pay-per-click advertising you may wish to promote your website with, ensuring that you put checks and balances in place to limit the maximum amount you're prepared to pay per click along with the maximum amount you're prepared to pay in any given period of time, normally by the day.

Data capture. When you have built your website try to ensure that you have a data capture mechanism in place, i.e.

a squeeze page, a free offer, free report, money off, or free shipping. Ensure your data capture of your customers' details are opted in so that you can email market to them with other offers

The steps and actions as listed above are very general and if you're not familiar with building your website it's worth either finding a web designer who can assist you at a cost that you're happy with or attending one of the many training courses that are held. You can get ahead by investing in yourself the time, money, and effort to do so. That's what I have done in order to create a business that has now turned over in excess of £1.6 million.

Don't want any stock? Become an affiliate

Affiliate marketing can be a great way to a passive income in your spare time with hundreds if not thousands of different opportunities available every day throughout the world. I very often come across two camps when talking about and looking at the affiliate marketing:

1. It's so complex and difficult but I could never work out how to write the HTML code to create the links or spend the time learning.

2. This is the easiest way to make money ever!

I will take the middle ground. It's not the easiest way to make money as there are a lot of very competitive affiliate marketers out in the marketplace. However, the way you can affiliate market has now changed and is changing all the time, which means you've got a lot of drag-and-drop or copy-and-paste linking which tends to make the whole process a lot easier as you do not have to write HTML code.

The easiest way I find to explain affiliate marketing is to carve yourself a niche image in writing product reviews, and linking that review to the affiliate link of the company that is selling the product paying you a commission. Affiliate commission varies wildly from just 4% on Amazon up to anything to as much as 75% on click bank. What you have to do is decide where you're going to carve your niche in writing your reviews.

Using something like WordPress to create your website and your review is fairly easy and straightforward. Linking through to the affiliate link on the sales page is also extremely easy. What you need to be aware of is who is searching for this product, what search terms are being used, how can you get yourself ranked fairly high in Google, and can you make money by using pay per click, SEO, or email marketing. As stated before, if you're going to use pay-per-click, ensure your results are many times more than the cost per click.

Whenever you sign up to an affiliate link, ensure you read their terms and conditions on how much commission you will be paid, when you will be paid, whether there are any clawback or lengthy delays due to the sellers' terms and conditions on refunds. Always monitor the affiliate link that you are promoting to ensure it's current and up-to-date. If you're dealing in areas such as technology, which can change rapidly, make sure you're always looking out for the next new model.

As with a standalone website the domain name URL is going to be vitally important to driving traffic. It's worth always trying to buy websites that are keyword rich to the search terms of the product you're going to sell. Always write your own reviews, do not plagiarise, copy-paste, or use manufacturers' descriptions unless you are fully authorised to do so. The only exception to that may be where you are using technical information that's key to the product's operating capacity.

It's worth checking out various online forums to ensure that any affiliates who are currently working with a company are not having problems or issues with payments, as the last thing you would want to be doing is spending two or three hours a day promoting the product and then wondering if the company is going to pay you on time, quickly, or ever. Do not get too hung up on the bad press in the forums, as some people just like to have a moan on a regular basis, although if there are a lot of people making comments then it's worth making a decision based on further analysis. That may even mean going directly to the company that you are thinking of providing an affiliate link to.

The majority of affiliate marketers will want to spend a little time on their marketing activities on a daily basis, and will normally be looking at products or services at a value of approximately £150 or $200 and above. There are many ways of finding products that have a captive audience, which will be covered in chapter 3.

Top Tip: For anybody looking at affiliate marketing, ensure you have a data capture mechanism on your website that allows potential customers to opt in so that you can forward them other affiliate links in the future. The easiest way to do this is to create a squeeze page on your WordPress site. There are a number of WordPress plug-ins that you can source to create these squeeze pages to ensure you capture their name and email address as a minimum. I have come across many affiliate marketers that just promote the product and never capture the details of the person making the purchase. It may add a little more time to put your review site together; however, if you manage to capture 100 email addresses that are opted in to receiving further opportunities from you, then you can start building a list which may well in time provide you with a regular passive income.

eBay

eBay is close to my heart as it's where it all started. Yet I hear a number of people who will protest to me that it's too expensive, they take too much money in fees, the customers never pay, they always leave negative feedback, it's only for selling second-hand used products, I can't guarantee that I will get the price I want for the item etc.

Well, I'm here to tell you it's not true. If any of the above is your perception of eBay then you need to relook at eBay and figure out why it's one of the best online selling marketplaces in the world today. I now sell new products at a price that is profitable. They are mainly sold on a buy-it-now basis and not through the auction, which is how eBay started and became known as the online auction site. We have no issues with customers paying and if we are getting any negative feedback then that will be because we have provided poor customer service. There are always exceptions...

Top Tip: When you open your first eBay account you will be asked for a unique eBay username that will be displayed to the world. Try to make it meaningful to the business or products you're going to sell. Treat your unique eBay username as either a keyword or a brand word, which means you will avoid such things as *fairydust14* or *gettingdrunktonight10,* as these will tend not to allow you to be taken seriously or professionally. This tip also applies when you're opening an eBay shop – you should ensure your shop name is meaningful.

Once you have completed opening your eBay account you have some choices to make depending on what you're going to sell, how many items you going to sell, and whether you want to upgrade to a shop.

A basic standard eBay account will allow you to sell any items; however, the fee structure for listing and final value fees will be higher than if you take one of the other packages available. Search for eBay shops to see the different price and the fee packages available.

Basic shop is the first point of entry and the one that most people will start off with, as it has some cost savings based on the fact that you will be paying a monthly fee. You do have to qualify to open your basic shop, which means you must have a minimum feedback score of 10 and the PayPal account must be verified.

Featured shop is the next one up, and again that has a different fee structure but is tailored towards sellers who may have multiple listings or multiple products selling in reasonable volume. When you're looking at the different structures it's worth doing the maths to ascertain which is the most cost effective based on the listing and final value fees. To open a featured shop you must be registered on eBay as a business and be PayPal verified with at least a 12-months' detailed sellers ratings of no less than 4.4 out of five. Normally this is fairly easy to achieve if you provide good customer service. For more detailed information on this go to eBay's customer service help pages, as the parameters may have changed since going to print.

Anchored shop is for those who have several thousand products or more with higher turnover in large volumes of sales going through the eBay system. Although like the featured shop you do have to qualify under eBay's rules that may change from time to time, so please refer to eBay's help pages for the latest detailed information.

Top Tip: Even if you do not wish to start trading yet, open an eBay account now and get your account verified by PayPal so they are linked, as this can take up to a week to 10 days to complete the PayPal verification process. Basically PayPal will take your details and they will pay some money into your account by direct debit and withdraw an amount. The value of these two transactions is always less than £1. You will then be asked to enter the differing amounts into a verification page to allow the account to become live.

Top Tip: If you have an old eBay account that you opened several years ago and have not used, then go through the process of resurrecting that account. Even if it has been inactive it may still go towards qualifying for the featured shop minimum period of 12 months. This will mean you can be up and running as a featured shop a lot quicker than if you were opening a brand new account.

If you already have an eBay account that has been doing well and you have kept it in good order, it's always worth contacting eBay customer support team as they may be able to help you progress quicker. This also applies if you're opening a second shop alongside your first shop. You may be able to do so straightaway if you have demonstrated over a period of time that your customer service metrics are excellent.

When you're selling on eBay you also have the opportunity to sell to many countries throughout the world, and depending upon the account type that you choose you may have very cost-effective ways of selling to the US, Canada, Australia, UK, Europe and others. There are opportunities for you to get your products into the hands of many customers worldwide; you just need the confidence to go there. People may want your product regardless of where you are in the world and they'll pay good money to get it there. To give you one example (and I have hundreds), we sold two Barbie body boards to somebody in Brazil. They weighed approximately two kgs, so were too big to use Royal Mail and had to go by DHL. They were a Christmas present and the cost to send them by DHL was £98 and the products were only £36. This customer paid nearly three times more in shipping because they wanted the product regardless of the shipping cost. And we got positive feedback too. The message is quite clear: don't limit your marketplace or opportunity to make a sale just because *you* think…. It's what the *customer* thinks that's important.

On eBay you can use video as well as pictures to show the customer your products. Video is becoming very important and we use two tools – one is a full-blown editing suite "Camtasia" and the other is by "Animoto". There are many other products on the market and some of them come free with some computers, so it's always worth searching the market place for something that's suitable for you. It's so simple to put video into your eBay listing, and it's one area that is being very little used. All you need to do is paste the HTML code from YouTube (or other eBay approved site) into your description on the HTML tab next to your standard description tab and it's done.

Fees and costs. Whatever you're selling on eBay you need to ensure that you cover your costs. As this varies from package to package, I have included in the purchase of this book a basic calculator that you can use for your own use as a free bonus. There is also another book in this series which goes into far more detail about eBay; it's called "The Book on How to Sell on eBay," and is available from www.thebookonhowtoselloneBay.com

Amazon

Amazon is a fantastic marketplace to sell in. Assuming you're selling products that are brand-new and have an EAN number (barcode), then you would be foolish not to sell through the Amazon marketplace. There are two caveats to that statement. If you're not prepared to give excellent customer service and you're out there to make a fast buck and don't care about your customers and are ripping them off, or if your products are so sensitively priced that there is very little margin in the profit, then don't bother with Amazon.

Amazon's customer service rules are really heavily stacked against the retailer. That said, if you are totally customer focused and totally customer driven to provide the most excellent service, then Amazon is definitely your marketplace. To give you an idea of why I say that, 70% of my turnover now comes from Amazon. Yes – 70% of my sales come from Amazon. Lots of people will tell you not to put all your eggs in one basket in case the basket falls over, and I agree with that.

However, Amazon is the brand that everybody recognises and trusts. Customers trust Amazon on the basis that they deliver and expect superb customer service. If an item is received damaged, it's returned. If it requires replacement, it's replaced. If the customer is not satisfied and just wants to return the item, the customer can return it. If the customer is not happy, they have an automated system called the A-Z guarantee which the customer can take issue with the Amazon marketplace seller. Eight times out of 10, Amazon will fall on the side of the customer if such a dispute arises.

So if Amazon is so demanding in the customer service department, you may ask, why sell there?

As previously stated, Amazon is a brand, when we get phone calls to our customer service team from Amazon customers they very often think they're calling Amazon and not an independent retailer. I think that's cool. I have excellent feedback through Amazon from my customers, and although Amazon would never allow me to say I'm an Amazon partner, just by the association of selling products and delivering exceptional service to my customers they are associating my business as being part of a global brand.

I'll say that again – a global brand. That's one of the most interesting and exciting aspects of selling through this company. Yes, it's expensive; the cost of sales with Amazon is approximately 17%. However, would I get the volume of sales through my stand-alone websites? No. How much would I have to spend on pay per click, SEO, and other general marketing initiatives to make up the shortfall of getting the volume sales I get through Amazon? A lot.

It's quick and easy to open an Amazon marketplace account. All you need to do is become registered, and there are various differently priced platforms for you to sell from. Therefore I urge you to go to Amazon's customer help pages, and a bit like eBay assess the package that is right for you.

As this is a general overview, I will give you some hints and tips on how to ensure you get your product noticed on Amazon. The very first thing to do with a new product is to put the barcode into Amazon and you will see if anybody else is selling it. This is crucial and I would urge you to do this before you purchase any product to sell on Amazon, and here is the reason.

The way Amazon works is that it automatically sorts the listing is based on the lowest price including shipping to get what's called the "buy button," located in the top right-hand corner of the page. This is fairly crucial to be able to get this position because most people when they purchase on Amazon do not click in to see all the other sellers who have the product. The majority just click the buy button.

Having the buy button is crucial for any Amazon retailer, so before you buy a product you want to know how many people are selling that product and what prices they are selling it for. Therefore, once you enter the barcode or description into Amazon, assuming it's listed, it will come up and you can have a look at all the retailers who are selling it and what price they're selling it for.

A good example is the following:

Product A		Product B	
Lowest listed internet price is £20 with free shipping and RRP of £30.00 so you sell at the competitive price of £20	20.00	Product selling price £30 plus shipping & packaging £4.00	34.00
15 other retailers also competitively selling the same product		Only one other seller at £30.00 plus shipping	
Product costs you	-10.00	Product costs you	-10.00
Postage	-2.50	Postage	-2.50
Packing	-1.50	Packing	-1.50
VAT/Taxes	-3.00	VAT/Taxes	-3.00
Total	-17.00	Total	-17.00
Net profit before fees	3.00	Net profit before fees	17.00
100 items purchased	1,000.00	100 items purchased	1,000.00
10 items lost or refunded	-170.00	10 items lost or refunded	-170.00
Profit potential if no further reductions	130.00	Profit potential if no further reductions	1,530.00

You also need to be aware of that where you have multiple sellers on a mainstream product you will see a price war, which normally sends the price tumbling so no one makes a good or sustainable profit. It's always better to find a niche where you can maintain a good margin.

So you can see quite easily that having a niche product where there are fewer sellers makes more sense rather than having a mainstream product where you have high amount of competition. This is where I see a lot of online retailers making big mistakes. I too have made those mistakes with some products and they are now discontinued lines, leaving everybody else to battle with the product and profit issue.

This is one of Amazon's strong points as far as customers are concerned – the more they drive the competition, the harder the competition will drive their prices downwards, so the consumer will always win. That said, it's exactly the market place you need to be in to find out if you can make a profit on the products you're selling. It may need a rethink on the products you sell so you can go for something a little more exclusive and niche. What you also have to be aware of is trends. If this is current in the trend today, would it still be there tomorrow? The other question is will the mass market take over, which may see your profit margin erode very quickly.

There is so much that I could go into in relation to selling on Amazon, along with some of the hints and tips on how to deal with competition, but I'm writing another book in the series titled "The Book on How to Sell on Amazon: www.thebookonhowtosellonAmazon.com

Top Tip: Keywords are essential. You need to do your market research to find the best keywords selling any product online, but especially on Amazon. The title of your product should be keyword rich. Also, if you go to edit your product details in the menu from the inventory page you will see a box with five lines, and each line can contain up to

50 characters of rich keywords. You may not want to believe this but many online retailers do not know that this exists.

> My eBay > Manage My Shop > Search Engine Keywords > Edit Keywords
>
> Enter new keywords to take place of those currently used on your page. Here are a couple of tips
>
> - please review the text on your Shop Front Page (for example, shop description, custom category names item title is and so on) to ensure that you are using appropriate keywords that are related to your page content.
> - Never use keywords that are not related to your page content will repeat the same keyword more than once. These are considered keyword spamming by search engines. Keyword spamming could affect your page ranking or cause your eBay shop page to be removed from the search engine indexes.
>
> | | New Custom Keywords | eBay Default |
> | --- | --- | --- |
> | Primary Keyword | Birthday presents wedding gifts | The name of your shop. |
> | Secondary Keyword 1 | Boy girl bride bridesmaid groom | The name of your category. |
>
> Please note that eBay may use only some of your custom keywords to generate your page title and Meta tags for search engine optimisation. For more information see Suggestions for Customising Keywords for Search Engines.

There are a number of other up-and-coming sites that are trying to challenge the marketplace that eBay and Amazon have throughout the world and they all have their little quirks.

Play.com

This site boasts some 15m subscribers, but how many are active is a different question. They also have a EU database but do not give any figures and have recently been taken over. It's being rebranded with what appears to be a major marketing focus on obtaining new retailers. They are making direct contact, and anybody with good customer service metrics and feedback with either Amazon or eBay is being invited to join play.com without going through any further checks. They operate mainly in the UK and Europe on the basis of a free post service and their charges in total are comparable to eBay.

There is a downside to play.com in that once you have uploaded your products, which take up to two weeks to become visible, you lose control of your product and listing, meaning any number of people can come alongside sell against you to drive the price down. It's an ideal marketplace if you're dealing with lower average transaction value products.

Ebid.net

With some 2.7m registered users it tries to function as an auction website like eBay used to. It does offer a fixed price lifetime seller package. Once your item is listed you cannot transfer it away from the site. It's small but viable, and although every sale counts, it's worth a look.

Quicksales.com.au

This Australian-based website claims to have over one million listings but does not appear to give statistics of how many registered subscribers. You can set up an item to be advertised for several months and link to other web stores for free, or sell on the store for as little as 2% final sales fee. There are no listing fees. This is a subscription website mainly targeted at the Australian audience, although you can sell anywhere in the world.

Bonanza.com

This American website appears to get a lot of traffic from Eastern Europe as well as in the United States, and has a lot lower final value fees, boasting as low as 3.5%. It offers several different plans that you can sign up to. If the United States is part of your target market it's worth a look as you can import your eBay listings onto Bonanza.com with a little input work from yourself and some assistance from their customer support teams.

Gumtree

Up-and-coming and having a lot of media attention in the UK, but what most people don't recognise is that Gumtree is part of eBay holding companies. It's a good way to trade your items at low risk and low cost. The marketing that they are doing is driving people to the site and I have certainly purchased a couple of bargains in the recent past.

Pinterest

This is a new one that looks very interesting and at the time of writing it's so new that I will have to put in more information on the website once we have more details and clarity on how it works for us from a retail point of view.

Your terms and conditions

Whichever website method you are going to use to sell your items you must ensure that you have a set of terms and conditions in line with the jurisdiction of the country you are trading in. In the UK it's known as the distant selling regulations; if you put into Google "distance selling regulations" you will be able to see in great detail what you need to do. You also need to consider how you're going to deal with returns – does the customer pay to return an item or do you pay for the return of an item? This needs to be extremely clear, especially with eBay and Amazon.

Your terms of sale should be kept fairly simple, easy to read, not too complex, and something the customer will be happy to agree to when making their purchase. There are a number of online sellers that present massive detailed legally written terms and conditions that the average customer may have difficulty understanding. This could lose you valuable sales. Try to keep your terms and conditions easy and simple to read and understand. There is lots of guidance around this online, but for a really good guide have a look at eBay and Amazon to get some ideas.

If you're selling to other countries you will also need to be aware of an import duty that your customer may have to pay, and it will need to be put in your terms of sale that they are responsible for the import duty on anything they purchase, along with ensuring your products comply with the country's customs regulations for import. As an example, you cannot import fishing bait catapults into Australia unless your customer holds a hunting license! The easiest way to ensure your products comply is by searching the country's customs website.

Chapter 3: Discovering What's Selling and How to Take Advantage

Whether I'm networking or giving a presentation, and sometimes coaching to people who are starting out or wanting to start out, the most frequent question I get asked is, "What should I sell?"

I cannot make up your mind on what you're going to sell; that's something only you can do. What I will say is to look towards products and services that you know something about or that you may be passionate about. A little bit of reverse engineering is required here, and rather than asking "What can I sell," take a step back and a deep breath and say to yourself "What do I know about, what am I passionate about?" Something to remember here is that everything that we tangibly touch has got to find its way to the marketplace for us to make the purchase and own it. That's where you should always start if you're new to retail selling online.

If you're already experienced online you may already have a number of suppliers that you source your product from, you may be importing directly from China or Asia, or you might even have a product in your hometown that you can take and you can sell for somebody else who is the local manufacturer. There is opportunity all around you. Sometimes you do not have to look too far; you just need to look.

Easy ways to find out what's selling now

If you're going down the route of affiliate marketing and are finding that products for sale is fairly easy, a few searches on Google and a look at what are the top sellers on Amazon will soon give you that information, and you'll be able to affiliate link to those products. The other way to find things is go to your local newsagent and look at some of the magazines. If you're into fashion, ask yourself what are the top trends in fashion at this moment? Can you capitalise or can you be affiliating/buying the brand; or identify what somebody will be copying and reproducing on a slightly different format. If you're into electronic gadgets, then again look at the magazines to see what's coming out and which one of the new models is going to be a top seller. Do some research on the Internet and find out who is selling something compatible or comparable.

Walk through your town. Pay attention to the shop windows and what's on display; is it seasonal or is it fashionable? What are the current news stories around products – maybe health, fitness, herbal medication, seasonal items for spring, autumn, summer or winter? All you need to do is look at what's current, think about what you're passionate or knowledgeable about, add those things together, and you'll have a vision of what you can sell.

Go for a walk

I spend many days at trade events walking around halls and looking for products that I believe will have a good market appeal, have low competition on the Internet, can be easily dispatched by post or courier, and that have a good profit potential after all costs. When I'm at these trade events I'm also looking for continuity of supply from the company from which I'm making the purchase. I'm also looking for things that I can repeat sell over a prolonged period of time.

That said, the sales agent on a trade stand approaches me and says there's a half-price offer whilst at the trade event today, never to be repeated. I will say "thank you very much, but I'm not interested." The reason is simple: if he has said that to me, he has said that to the other hundred people whom he has approached. That product will get taken by a small number of people, and you will then see it appearing online and the price being reduced with margins eroded as people struggle to sell the item. There are always exceptions but I have not yet found one.

It's fairly easy to find trade events – a search on the Internet will easily tell you where they are and the dates, and once you subscribe to their website you will get very regular emails informing you of new events. For serious business owners these events are a must because you can get so much information from the people who attend the events, whether it's other retailers online or whether it's from the agents and staff who are on the trade stands. They are normally so keen to sell that they will give you a lot of information that you would normally not be privileged to have obtained, and will find it extremely useful.

TRADE SHOW EVENT SCHEDULE PLANNER

PROJECT PHASE	STARTING	ENDING	PROJECT PHASE	STARTING	ENDING
UK GIFT FAIR	[Select Date]	[Select Date]		[Select Date]	[Select Date]
EU TRADE FAIR	[Select Date]	[Select Date]		[Select Date]	[Select Date]
CHINA TRADE EVENTS	[Select Date]	[Select Date]		[Select Date]	[Select Date]
USA TRADE EVENTS	[Select Date]	[Select Date]		[Select Date]	[Select Date]

(Calendar grid for January through December)

Use the "sell anything" approach

There is another very successful way of doing things and that is to purchase end of line, job lots, clearance, or High Street shop returns or overstocks. A lot of these are sold through brokers and sometimes they can be broken down into pallet lots. The way this normally works is the seller of the stock (the broker) will tell you what the RRP (recommended retail price) is for that product and then they will offer you a discount represented by a percentage of the RRP value.

A couple of notes of caution if you want purchase through this method. You need to be sure that the clearance price your purchasing the items at is low enough for you to sell them in the marketplace. I will give you a quick example:

- RRP was £10 per item for a toaster. The broker has one hundred toasters available with a total RRP value of £1,000.

- You are offered toasters at 20% of the RRP = £200 (£2 each). This sounds like a good deal to you.

- Your local big discount retailer is selling the same item at a 50% discount of RRP (£5 each).

So what are you going to do regarding shipping?

Therefore you have got to decide using the cost analysis calculator whether you can compete and make money.

Toaster	Price
Cost	2.00
Tax	0.40
Selling fees	0.75
Packaging	0.80
Cost	3.95
Shipping	4.00
Total	11.90

So after doing a rough calculation the total cost to you before shipping to sell them online may be £3.95, leaving you with just over a pound profit. However, if the shipping for this item is four pounds then you're trying to sell the item at nearly the RRP price. You can position this another way by advertising the product with the normal retail price plus shipping is £14 and discounted with free shipping to £8.95. Then you're making your item look more attractive. If you're selling the item at £3.95 plus shipping it starts to look more expensive to the customer.

In this situation I would be looking to purchase the consignment at around 7% to 10% of the RRP, as that would give me more margin to put a good deal together for my customer. So the tip here is quite simple do not get carried away with the initial offer of discount against the RRP. You may need to negotiate a bigger discount.

If you're going to go down this method of retailing so you're not specialising in any particular niche areas. The fact that you're going down the discount online retail route will mean that this will become your brand and you may have difficulty in removing/changing your identity from that branding at a future date.

Discover your niche

Lots of people discover their niche, and some of them may actually make the items themselves as a craft or hobby. This can quite easily be turned into a business. If you have such a hobby or craft then going online makes perfect sense, and a good source of information to help you will be your local chamber of commerce. They will be able to assist you with growth strategies, and there may be some local business partners that you can team up with as you may require a small workforce or small premises as the business grows.

Growing your niche from your passion, craft, or hobby may mean you are doing something that you love and that financial return is not as important as the satisfaction of selling your product. Whilst you are a small operator that is fine; at some point, when it's a business, you may need to try and separate your heart from your head.

Chapter 4: How to Achieve Quick Credibility and Positive Feedback Ratings

This chapter assumes that you are new to eBay, Amazon, or any of the other online websites, and you need to build your feedback and ratings quickly within the structure of the online marketplace. This can also work if you have a credibility or feedback system on your standalone web store. It's worth pointing out initially that some of these tactics may be a little left of centre and not seen to necessarily work within the spirit of the provider.

What your customer is looking for?

Before you list or purchase any product it's worth having a look to find out what people are looking for and wanting to purchase. On eBay there's a great way to find out what some of the top sellers are selling a lot of. If you click onto the product you will normally see the quantity available, and next to that figure you will see the number of units sold.

That number is an active link, so when you click on that link it will actually show you how many have been sold and on what dates. If that particular seller is using the bid and offer system in eBay it will tell you the price that has been accepted for each purchase. This little tip is not well known but it's a fantastic way to do some research on your ideas.

You can then go to Amazon and have a look at the top-selling items, and that will give you some numbers that will help you get a feel for the product's popularity. Once you have identified the product that you're going to sell and you know your buying price, you then have a couple of decisions to make:

Am I going to sell this at no profit to build up some ratings quickly?

Am I going to sell this at a loss as a marketing strategy to drive my ratings up quickly?

On the basis that you have made a decision – and let's say you have decided you need to build 100 pieces of feedback with 100% rating for a short period of time – you need to plan how you're going to implement it. Work on the basis that only 40% of people will leave you any feedback (as a rough rule of thumb it can be up to 60% on eBay and less than 30% on Amazon). This may mean you need to sell 250 items at the price that you have settled for to get to your target.

Your customer is going to be looking for price, speed of delivery, and customer service. As this is going to be a price driven marketing campaign you will need to ensure your total price including shipping is a lot more attractive than any of your competitors. It may be that you need to make a loss until you've reached your target feedback and then put your prices up. So ensure you plan your marketing campaign adequately.

Take action every time

First piece of action is to get your items listed as soon as possible. If using eBay ensure that you're selling it as a buy-it-now item, not an auction item. Do not use the offer option, as this will drive your price down further. As soon as you've got the item listed, go to the next step, and pack the first batch so that all you have to do is put the address and postage label onto the item as it sells. This can save you hours of packing.

Then ensure that you are checking very regularly for sales. The moment a sale drops in dispatch it immediately, and where necessary pay the difference for next day delivery without this being advertised in your sales page. For example, if a customer buys it at 2 PM on Monday and it's delivered at 10 AM on Tuesday, you've just got your feedback and they will be blown away with your service.

This method requires you to be organised with a marketing strategy that implies urgency for the customer to buy at that price and for you to deliver very quickly to get great feedback. The minute you have got to your target feedback then you can revise the item's selling price and increase accordingly, or, of course, simply carry on until you have sold all your stock.

Whilst looking at this as a strategy you may decide to purchase stock specifically for this exercise, so that you have a site that has all the correct feedback metrics you require to enable you to sell the other items that you actually wish to sell. The feedback will not change but the items can change, so it's a very good tactic to use to get you noticed very quickly.

Sell to friends and family

This method may be a little bit of a "black art." I do not advocate this method and you may not feel comfortable with it; however, I have included it because I know people out there who do this. List your product/s and request your friends and family to purchase the product through their own eBay and Amazon accounts. They in turn leave you positive feedback, and whether the sale is totally completed or reversed and refunded or they pay online and you send the money back is fairly irrelevant. Because unless a complaint is made there is very little chance that this tactic will be spotted. There are exceptions, such as if you were to sell and refund everything. This one is very useful where somebody only needs ten pieces of feedback on eBay so that they can go to the next level to open an eBay shop.

Invest in yourself

Purchase an existing online business that already has the feedback and customer service metrics in place from a proven track record over a period of time. You may or may not wish to purchase the stock that that business selling; that is a discussion between you and the seller. There are many businesses for sale through business transfer agents and even on eBay where you can take over an existing account and perhaps move it to the next level or just trade through their previous performance and make a better job of it. This may also be used by your accountant as tax strategy for the business.

There will be costs incurred in this and it must be seen as an investment. It's always worth taking legal advice before you embark on this as a strategy, but it's a very quick way of buying into the marketplace and then putting promotion around the new stock you are introducing. Or, it may be that you purchase the existing stock of the seller and decide to aggressively sell it in to the marketplace to clear it, making a small return on your investment.

Chapter 5: The Five Worst Mistakes and How to Avoid Them

During the course of this book you have probably gathered that I'm quite an advocate of good customer service. I drive my team to deliver excellence and occasionally it costs money to put something right. We are all capable of making mistakes, but as long as you learn from the mistakes then at least you will not repeat them in the future. Sending the wrong product to a customer is very annoying to both parties, but the way you deal with the solution can turn that customer into a lifelong repeat spending advocate of your web shop. Never forget that the opportunity to put things right can lead to repeat business and new business because of your actions. However, if you can't be bothered and you don't care, then please don't get into the business.

1. Not talking to your potential customers

Every question a customer poses to you is a valid question in that customer's mind. No matter how ridiculous you think the question is or the fact that you already provided the answer in your listing is an irrelevance to the way you handle an answer that customer's question. Whenever you get a question, just pause for a few seconds to ensure that you have not created confusion in your listing. You may fully understand the details and the complexities of the listing. You may know your products so well that you're using an internal language to that of your industry that your customer does not understand. Also, your customer may be from a different background or culture, or may have issues in reading. So never stop communicating with your customer regardless of how you will personally feel about his or her question.

The speed at which you communicate can mean the difference between a sale and no sale. Try to answer all emails within a few hours, or at least within 24 hours. With technology today there is no excuse; you can have questions sent to your mobile phone or to your laptop. You may be out of town but there will be absolutely nothing stopping you going into an Internet cafe or a library and using their services.

Communication is the key to your success. If a customer has a problem with an item that they have purchased or the payment mechanism did not work for some reason, take ownership of that problem and provide them with a solution. They will be extremely happy to recommend your services and give you feedback.

When you have an item that requires replacement, you need to decide how far you're going to inconvenience the customer. In my business our rule of thumb is if the customer sends a photograph of the damaged item, I will send a replacement immediately. If I believe I require the item back because of it having a manufacturer's defect I will also send a returns label with the replacement item so that the customer is not inconvenienced any further than necessary. You may also want to consider spending the extra money it will cost to have the replacement item delivered the next day. Again your values and requirements for your business will help you decide. I find that when customers get that level of service along with a telephone call or a follow-up email to ensure everything is okay they will remember and come back time and time again.

If you're working from home and your telephone calls are sent to an answering service, you must ensure that the service comes over as professional and leaves a message that states when the customer can expect a return call from you. This is called managing the customer's expectations. There is nothing worse than leaving a message for somebody and by the time they phone you six to eight hours later you're fuming about the lack of customer service. Whereas if you were to say "We return customer calls between 6pm and 8pm daily," then you have managed that customer's expectations when they telephoned and left your message at 10am.

Where you have emails coming in from customers, use an auto responder to send an instant reply which will give them some specific detail about when they can expect a personal reply in line with the message on your answering machine.

The majority of customers that you will come across are honest, reliable, and just want their issue sorted out. That does not mean to say you're not going to get Mr or Mrs Angry on the end of the telephone or writing emails in a defamatory way. If you do have customers like this and you're selling through eBay, Amazon, or any one of the others platforms, you have the option to report that customer for further investigation by their customer service teams. They will never tell you what the outcome is; however, I'm aware of customer's accounts being closed or cancelled, having warnings put against them, and where they have left any negative or abusive feedback it has been removed.

Amazon and eBay, although both very customer focused, are also focused on protecting their merchant sellers from the very small percentage of customers who try to benefit from the system in either abusive or fraudulent ways. Great customer service starts immediately they place the order and they get the automated emails thanking them for their order and advising them of the progress in shipping the order.

2. Over pricing and under delivering

There are a number of people selling on eBay and Amazon who have decided they will put extra money on the postage and packaging charges so they can make a little bit extra. This is short sighted for a number of reasons. The customer is not so stupid as to not to be able to work out what a fair shipping price is. I had a recent example where somebody was selling an electronic whiteboard in an auction on eBay and it stated the carriage cost for this whiteboard would be £50. I bid for this item and I won it; however, they lived so close to me I was able to collect it and not pay the carriage. Therefore I purchased an item that I needed but could sell for at least ten times the purchase cost (which was £32) and would be able to ship it within the UK for less than £10. So although the seller made a sale they did not get anything like the price they could have done if they had not been so greedy on shipping.

If you're just an occasional seller, then you may not know where to find cost-effective shipping. All you need to do is put a search into Google, something along the lines of "I want to send a parcel to..." It could be UK, USA, Australia, Europe – it doesn't matter where because you will get companies like parcel 2go.com, parcel2ship.co.uk, or fastlaneinternational.com. These types of companies are basically parcel brokers and they are selling you space with carriers such as DHL, FedEx, UPS, Parcelforce, Citylink, and so many more. When you find these companies online they will ask you for the weight and the dimensions of the parcel. Simply complete those details and you will be given a page of quotes for all the different carriers that they use so that you can make an informed choice and get the best deal for your customer.

Top Tip: Before you list your product work out the shipping cost by using the above methods so that you do not get caught out by selling an item and not charging the correct shipping amount. It's also worth remembering that the quotes you will see will be net of VAT so you will need to add the VAT to the price for UK and European shipping. However, if you're shipping from the UK outside of Europe then there will be no VAT on shipping but there may be customs duty payable by your customer at point of entry to their country.

Assuming you're reading this in the UK then you may be using Royal Mail or a similar service for other countries. A lot of people still going queue up at the post office and pay the post office counter rate. This is in effect full recommended retail price of postage and the most expensive way for you to send your packets and parcels. To bring down the cost go to Royalmailonline.co.uk and purchase your postage online; this will save you anywhere up 10% or more of the post office counter cost. All you need to do then is print it off, attach it to your parcel and drop it off at the post office. Just doing this will save you a lot of money.

The next step is to look at franking machines; however, a word of caution – be careful of getting into a long-term contract with a franking machine company unless you know that you will fulfil enough orders to warrant keeping the franking machine contract. Basically with franking machines you're preloading the machine with postage that you're buying in advance, so it's a little bit like a pay-as-you-go mobile phone contract.

If your volume of sales is going to be fairly large then look at creating a business account with Royal Mail and take advantage of the tiered discounted rates that they apply for volume sellers. If you're spending in excess of £15,000 per annum then you will also be entitled to free daily collections. If you're spending is lower than that amount then they normally charge you an annual fee, which is presently about £500.

One of the best ways of getting good feedback is to get the items out in the post as quickly as possible, same day as purchase if at all possible; however, on your website you will probably state either two to three days or three to five days delivery. Just think how great your customer feels if they get it next day or within 48 hours. This will not only make you look efficient but it will also help the customer to give you some immediate feedback.

3. Poor packaging

Nobody likes receiving a parcel in an old tatty box covered with tape wrapped in a black thin polythene dustbin liner with a piece of paper taped, ripped, and torn with appalling hand written felt marker address details. This just does not look professional, especially when you have given a wonderful description of the item that you have sold them. As part of our business we send parcels for the general public and what I just described above we see on a regular basis. In fact just recently we had a customer bring us a used laptop they had sold on eBay that they wanted to post and they had stuck the address label to the top of the laptop and thought it would get to the customer with no problem!

Invest in some good quality packaging. You can buy it all online, and you need to add the cost into your price to make sure you making a profit, although packaging is not expensive if you purchase it correctly. A tip here is not to buy it from high-street retailers as their profit mark-up will be higher than the online sellers.

A clean Jiffy bag or a nice new cardboard box lined with bubble-wrap, and good quality brown tape with a neat self-adhesive address label with return contact details in the top corner make the recipient feel as if you care about the product that you're sending. If you have purchased anything from Amazon you will know that when that package arrives it's been packed and handled with care and you feel happy opening your purchase. Your customers need to feel the same when they open their purchase from you.

Top Tip: Make a flyer with an offer, maybe 10% off your next purchase or freepost or even a free gift. Do not lose this valuable opportunity to allow the customer to come back to you directly and make a further purchase. If you're selling through Amazon or eBay and your flyer is directing them to your web shop and the second purchase is made from that web shop, then you have not accrued any fees to eBay or Amazon. So that 10% discount has really cost you nothing.

4. Not taking advantage of great photos

I recently saw an item on sale on eBay with the picture of the item taken on the kitchen table. In the background were the kitchen cupboards and various items of crockery and food on the work surface, and there were also stains and marks on the table that did not look good.

Would I seriously want to buy that item?

Can I actually see the item correctly in the picture?

An example picture to illustrate

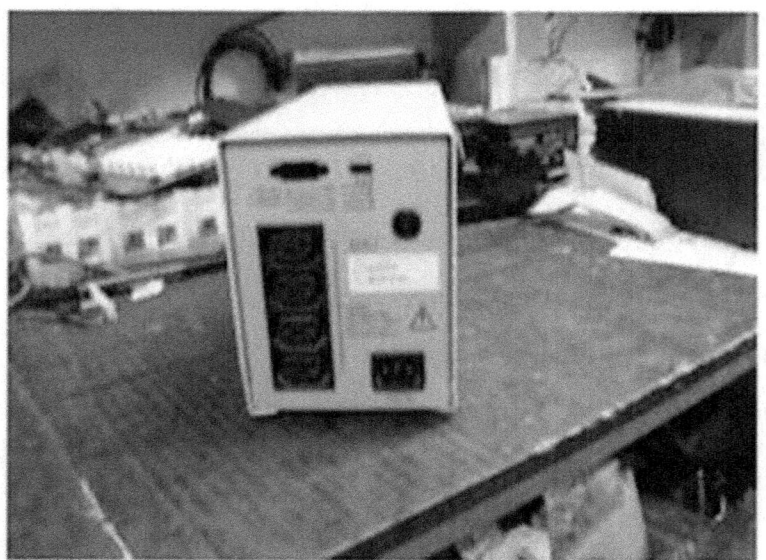

Top Tip: Use a white background, which can be a sheet or a piece of board. Take a good photograph of the item. If the item has serial numbers and manufacturers reference numbers, take a close-up photograph of those, place that as your second photograph. If your item has any marks or flaws then take a picture of those too.

Don't include borders, text or artwork on the picture

All text and borders should be removed to create a cleaner experience for buyers. Watermarks can be used to protect copyright.

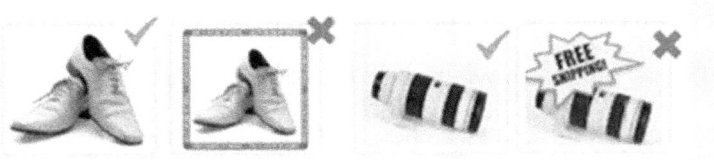

Make sure you have good light on the item. If you're selling a lot of items you may wish to purchase a light box with a set of special lights to ensure that your pictures will be crisp and clear. Make sure there is nothing in the background that will distract the purchaser's attention from making the purchase of the item, or from making judgements about you the seller.

When you're taking your picture if the file is in a large format use picture resizing software. Most new computers now come with it preloaded, so that it will not take a long time to upload when your potential customer is searching the Internet. Personally, all of my pictures get resized to 800×800. Then you need to crop your picture so that you can show the item off at its best while also noting any flaws that the item may have.

Always be mindful that your customer is purchasing the picture first and your written description second. As a little bit of an exercise, next time you wish to make a purchase go online and note how you search. How long do you study a photograph before you click on that photograph to either make it larger or to get the written detail? Whilst you're searching make some notes, and if you're in a place where you're able to observe how other people search products use that information when you're listing your own products.

5. Shaky or unprofessional video

It's forecast that over the next few years streaming video is going to be the best way to get your products on top of the search engines. Google already likes video but you've got to know how to use it to its best advantage. As with taking pictures, a shaky video doesn't look professional, so you need to invest in a little bit of equipment.

When you're showing an item that would benefit from a 360° view, then a little turntable makes all of the difference, and a five second video may just allow the buyer to press the buy button against that of your competitor. Videos are now easy to make with mobile phones, reasonable quality cameras and free online software; all you need is a little imagination and a few extra minutes. It can make the difference between a sale or no sale.

I use a lot of Animoto video for my purposes – it's quick, easy and effective, and if I'm showing a range of products I will compile up to 20 still photographs into Animoto so that the customer can see a very professional image of the rest of the product range. They also supply royalty free music.

There are many free packages available and there are some that also are chargeable. You need to decide how much value you're going to place on using video and video editing in order to drive your products hard and fast in the retail market. My other favourite is a software called Camtasia, which allows me to use music with voice over to make mini commercials to help sell the products.

Presently at the time of writing, Amazon does not allow us to use video on their site. However, eBay will allow video in the listings, as this is not heavily used that moment it actually means that you get higher rankings in the searches where you have used video and where you have titled the URL to the video with keywords.

Top Tip: Whenever you use photographs or video ensure that you rename the video or photograph using keywords that will help the search engines find the product. Lots of people leave the details of the image so it may read something like *img245867* instead of *Sony Cybershot W120 Camera*. Therefore if I'm looking for a Sony cybershot camera, the image with the renamed title is going to be searchable. So the chances of that seller having their listing come up high in the rankings is very good.

Chapter 6: The Shocking Truth Behind Free Shipping

What is free shipping, really?

DHL, FedEx, UPS, Royal Mail, all provide a free shipping service to us the retailers!

If only this were true. The bottom line is "There is no free shipping." I will repeat that: "There is no free shipping." It's a myth. The cost of the shipping is always calculated into the selling price of the item. And yet customers love the idea of having something free. They see free shipping as a bonus and an acceptable giveaway by the retailer.

If you were to say to a customer, "I will give you this free toaster but I want you to pay £25 shipping," the customer would think you were ripping them off. And yet if you say "I will give you this £25 toaster with free shipping," the customer will think you're being very generous. The fact that they could buy it for £19 at the local electrical store is irrelevant because they are seeing the higher price with the perception of an acceptable free offer.

Whenever you look at the online adverts for products you can often find higher-priced items that claim to have free shipping listed higher than the lower-priced item with shipping to be added. EBay, especially at the moment, likes free shipping, and to sellers with shops there are incentives for you to offer free shipping.

Why offer free shipping?

The customer perception that they are having a bargain or getting something free is a massive bonus to that customer. I have a number of products for which I offer free shipping on in order to drive more traffic to our online shop. It's a well known strategy within the world of retail to allow the customer to perceive that they are having something of added value free of charge.

We have feedback from customers that will say, "Thank you for the free shipping," and yet we have still had to pay the carrier to take the parcel to the customer. If you want to sell on play.com then all of your items must be perceived as having "free shipping"; therefore you are allowed to add the shipping cost into the final selling price. Now with play.com what you have to remember is they will charge you a final value fee as a commission when it's sold. Therefore when you're working out your item price you need to allow a percentage to be added to the shipping cost to offset their commission.

We can argue and debate the true value and meaning of free shipping all day long; however, it's here to stay, with the customers perceiving they're getting added value. Therefore, it works to use it and test it on your products. If you've got products where you have a lot of competition, that's a perfect item to test the free shipping scenario. You will be surprised how many sales you will get purely because it says free shipping. Another way to look at this is that many people will see something like the following: item price £25 with free shipping or they may see item price £19 shipping £4.98. The perception is that either the shipping looks expensive so I will go for the free shipping option, or mathematics was never their strong subject and they cannot work out the fact that the item with the shipping works out cheaper.

How to calculate free shipping

This is fairly straightforward. First of all I would suggest you have a look at competitors in the marketplace and see what they're offering, and then use a table something like this:

Free Shipping	Cost	Chargeable Shipping	Cost
Toaster	10.00	Toaster	10.00
Tax	2.00	Tax	2.00
Packing	1.50	Packing	1.50
Online Fees	2.50	Online Fees	2.50
Total	16.00	Total Cost	16.00
Shipping	4.98	Shipping charged	4.98
Total Cost	20.98	Shipping charged	4.98
Sale Price	25.00	Sale Price	19.00
Profit	4.02	Profit	3.00

If you offer something with free shipping on the basis that the customer uses the perception that they are getting the bonus, you may make an extra 25% net profit on this transaction. The above example is that purely for the purposes of this book; you need to apply your scenario, which will be different every time to each item you're selling, ensuring you have researched your competitors to ascertain what they are doing. It may be that you can get a good deal on the shipping and can even make extra profit.

Take advantage of free shipping

The key to using the free shipping model is to know and work out your cost – the actual cost per item to you down to the last penny. You also need to work out what your stock loss or refund rate will be. As one of the downsides of offering free shipping is that if you have to refund a customer for non-delivery, damage, or they return it because they have changed their mind, you will be refunding the full value of the transaction, so although you can earn more income from the free shipping model you may also have higher refund costs. Most items will have an industry average for refund rates; I work on 2% for my business. Yours may be different.

Use the initiative to drive sales to capture your competitor's marketplace from a position of strength, ensuring that you have the total cost base of the item that you're sending along with an allowance for refunds and replacements to create your net profit return. It's worth noting that if you're selling a product that's in a very competitive market, the buying power of larger organisations may mean that their offer to that marketplace cannot be beat and you're going to be selling a product against them with very low profit margins. If that's the case, ask yourself the questions, Is this worth selling? Can I make any money? Will I sell enough volume to generate other income streams from selling this product? Will it return an overall profit?

Free shipping is a great marketing tool. Use it to its maximum effect and ensure that you capitalise on the opportunity, especially when you're selling into a crowded market. If you're in the market to build lists of customers or potential customers then using the free shipping tool may be very valuable as a long-term strategy; or if you want to build page rankings or great customer feedback this strategy can certainly work, and if you remember to over deliver and under promise your feedback ratings will climb higher and quicker.

Chapter 7: How to Find Stock in a Crowded Marketplace

If, like me you have attended various seminars, you will be fairly familiar with the question that some people asked on a regular basis: What is your "WHY" and is it big enough for you to actually do something about it? Or are you one of life's dreamers that thinks that it would be a nice thing to do get round to one day? The reason that I put this in is because that will determine which part of your plan you need to go to next. It will also depend on how urgently you need to realise your "WHY."

Do you have an urgent requirement for cash?

At this point I'm assuming that you're not in business yet or you're in business and it's starting to go backwards and there is an urgent need to generate cash relatively quickly. The first thing I would suggest that you do is to take a look at everything you own. And plan to dispose of the 80% of the items that you own that you never use, never wear, or have sat on a shelf, in the garage, or a drawer, wherever it may be without being looked at or used. Yes, you will have some items of genuine sentimental value. But other than those genuine items, *sell everything else*. Just do it. Sell the 80% of items you own that you will never ever use again, and in the case of some books, never opened. Put them onto eBay or similar and just get whatever you can for them. The same rules apply to make sure the photographs are excellent, your description is accurate and informative, if there are any flaws then they are detailed in full, and when your purchaser completes the transaction make sure you send it immediately.

If you're at this stage, you can also ask your friends and family for any items they no longer require so that you can sell for them on their behalf with an arrangement that you can keep some of the proceeds. Finding items to sell in your own environment is easy – you just have to look.

If you're in business and you hold a lot of stock, the same rule applies. Look at the stock that you have. When was the last time you sold any of it? Is it now obsolete, out of date, out of fashion? Rough rule of thumb – if you owned a piece of stock for more than 12 months then its value is probably less than 5% of the cost price. On that basis anything you make is a bonus, so just sell it and turn it into cash. Any decent accountant will be able to create a tax write-off once you get back on your feet so that you will be able to get something extra from what you sold.

Once you managed to clear some of the items that you no longer need, you can then start investing the proceeds in new stock or new opportunities to grow your existing business or start your new business. You should be able to create enough capital to purchase a new line of stock or perhaps some training if you want to get into, say, affiliate marketing.

Sell products from your home or garden shed

One of the best ways to start your business from scratch is to use your home, garden shed or garage to initially purchase and store products. However, if you're doing this with a local supplier it will be a good idea to see if you can go daily to collect the goods that you have sold from the previous day. This way you will keep your cash flow fairly smooth and it will also mean that you will always be buying on a "just-in-time basis."

You will find that a lot of the big multiple retailers operate their stock rotation on a just-in-time basis by ensuring that whatever has sold that day is replenished overnight. This always helps keep the cash flow fairly tight and means that less space is required for storage. Trying to find a local business supplier for your initial sales is a very useful and helpful exercise.

If you do purchase large amounts of stock and are storing them at your home, ensure that you have adequate insurance cover in case of loss.

One of my close friends came up with the idea of selling handmade fishing items from his garden shed and has built quite a successful business. He makes the items himself, and his sons are also now involved in the production. They sell them throughout the UK quite easily, making a few pounds. So you do not need to necessarily look at the big businesses because there are always buyers for locally produced or handmade items. Check out your local cash-and-carry, I have even come across people who've gone to the discount retailers to purchase stock from there and resold it on eBay.

Other areas to check out are auction houses, local car boot sales, and bankrupt stock. Look for local businesses that are closing down, and if they are an independent business go talk to the owner as they may be keen to do a deal. I have done several all very profitably for both parties. Keep your eye on the local press to see who is having a major sale, as you may be able to purchase product in the sale and sell it for more money.

Expanding your existing retail business

If you're simply expanding your existing retail business to an online position, then you're probably going to have ines of credit with existing suppliers. Once you've managed to gauge the opportunity of selling your items online, it may be a useful exercise to check out with your supply chain the continuity of supply. Also, do you know whether you're purchasing at the cheapest price possible? You may need to ask. I know a number of businesses that have built up solid relationships with their supply chain but never ask for a discount for fear of ruining the relationship. If you're going to increase your business, you want your buying price to be as low as possible. I always ask what the highest discount available is for a product and how many of them I need to purchase to get that discount. This enables me to focus on whether I can get to that level if I have a market that will take the stock.

It's worthwhile checking out to ascertain if you're purchasing from the right person. There may be several agents in the chain, all of whom are taking a cut. If that's the case you owe it to yourself to see if you can go direct to the manufacturer/importer and cut out as many of the agents as possible. You may need to increase your purchasing power to do that, and if that's the case look to see if you have a friendly competitor that may well benefit from you working together on joint orders.

Before expanding your business online you must do your research. Using Google Analytics and/or Google Trends will tell you how much historical activity there was the marketplace for the product that you are offering. You need to know how many people are searching; you also need to know what the keyword search terms are for your product. All of this is available to you free through Google. If you do not have the time or experience to do that yourself it can be outsourced to a third party who will provide you with a report.

Points worth noting: if you're going to outsource, then ask for quotes first, and get a minimum of three. If you're part of a networking group for the chamber of commerce, speak to them to find someone in your local area and providing that service. The other alternative is for you to use O Desk, Elance, or a similar site, and you will be able to outsource this at a reduced cost. You can find out about outsourcing by searching the Internet or by purchasing my new book, which covers this topic in more detail.

Growing your website in different directions

Assuming your business is already up and running, you might be looking for new and different items to sell. If you have a speciality or niche that you are working in, then ask the wholesaler, visit relevant trade events, and speak to importers. They are also looking for commission earnings and they may well be able to source items which you can have your own label or brand, which means nobody else can sell them in the marketplace.

This may be a big step. It's a very good step to make if you have a product that currently sells very well with a good profit retention. What you need to do is then find an agent who can get the exact same product made but with your branding and/or bar code so that nobody has the opportunity to directly copy it. It may be your present supplier is able to bring the line in as a "special" just for you with minor tweaks to differentiate it from a mainstream product.

The trick with this type of opportunity is to ensure that you maximise the sales potential through very focused keyword analysis and high-quality photography along with videography. You are now building your own brand on your own website and of course you're able to create these products to sell in the Amazon marketplace, eBay, and potentially worldwide.

If you don't want to go down that road you can always look for other items, i.e., buying the trade press. One useful source of information is a magazine called "The Trader," which is available in the UK at most newsagents and also has an online presence. Another useful way of finding stock is through the brokers who deal in large volume stock trading. These may be lots of several thousand items that have belonged to bankrupt companies, have been left at the dockside through unfulfilled orders, or were refused orders from multinational retailers whose deadlines have not been met by the importer, who at this stage may be desperate to turn the investment into cash via liquidators and recovery agents. I get offered on a daily basis stock from all around the world that is classed as distressed stock and very often is available at extremely low prices.

Chapter 8: Is Your Web Shop a Needle in the Internet Haystack?

Your business – in fact every business – starts at the bottom rung of the ladder. Now you may want to name your business something really fancy that is valuable to you. You may be thinking "I need to be a brand so I'm going to have this wonderful logo with a wonderful name that means a lot to me." Remember that it's likely the cherished name means absolutely nothing to anybody outside of your immediate circle. I will argue that once you have got some sales you have tested the market with sound knowledge that you can make profits, and only then should you start worrying about fancy names or logos. Let's face it: if you spend thousands of pounds on your image but neglect your sales strategy, you will have a wonderful image at the time you declare bankruptcy.

What's in a domain name?

In my view your domain name should say something about what you do or what you sell. This book is called "The Book on How to Sell Online" and the domain name for the website is www.TheBookOnHowToSellOnline.com. In other words, I have left you some clues in the title. Therefore when you purchase your domain name find some keywords that describe your business, the product, or the service that you are selling. If you're only looking for customers in your hometown or within your county then you may well wish to include the area name within the title. This way you're telling potential customers your location and the service or products you will supply are contained within the keywords, which are easily found on the search engines.

There are many web hosting and domain name companies out there. I tend to use 1and1, Hostgator, and GoDaddy to source my domains. Most of these companies will rent you the domain name on an annual basis for as little as £2.99 per annum. Different ones have different packages depending on whether you require .co.uk, .com, or any other country prefix that you may be trading in. It's worth remembering that if you're trading and only selling products in the UK then it's advisable to purchase a domain name with .co.uk, whereas if you're planning to go international then you may wish to look at .com. If you're targeting specific countries you may wish to purchase .au you for Australia, .ca for Canada, .fr for France, or .de for Germany, and the list can go on. If you're planning to selling to non-English-speaking countries then it would also be worthwhile to ensure that you purchase the domain name using the correctly translated title in that chosen language.

The make up of the domain name will contain a string of keywords that will be crucial to your being found on the Internet. Once you have your domain name set up and you have built your website or web shop, you want to make sure that it's keyword rich within the page titles, the product or service titles are in bold and underlined, and any pictures or video have the correct string of keywords to help the search engines rank you higher. Once you've found your domain name it's worth considering purchasing other similar domain names if you believe that there may be competition within the marketplace and that your competitors may be able to steal some of the potential income by driving traffic to domains with similar sounding names. It's a small investment that's worth considering to protect your sales channel.

Top Tip: If your name is Peter Smith with a business in Croydon and you're going to sell reconditioned motorcycle parts, do not call yourself www.PeteSmithspares.co.uk, as this does not tell anybody any information about your business. You may consider calling yourself something like www.reconditionedmotorbikesparesCroydon.co.uk, or if you were shipping throughout the UK you may drop the Croydon, or even better have two domain names with one for your local business and another that points to your main web shop, which gives the impression of nationwide or international delivery services. Of course if you were in a niche market you might want to use the name of the bike as in Norton, BSA, Honda, etc.

Have the right keywords

How do you find the right keywords? This is both an art and an ever-changing science. Because Google regularly changes the way their search engines find rank and rate websites and products, it can be difficult to find that "magic bullet" guaranteed to propel your site to the top of searches. What you can do at the moment is find out what the trends are that are relevant to the way the search engines operate today and then you need to keep up-to-date with those changes to stay current.

First, let's talk about keywords. Below is a quick summary of what a keyword is.

WHAT is a keyword?

A keyword is any word or short phrase that describes a website topic or page.

The more a keyword is used by searchers and websites the more attraction power it has.

If you want your website to attract searchers, you need to use strong keywords in your website titles and website text. These brief words should realistically identify and describe your site.

The Google Keyword Tool is the world standard for webmasters' research to test search words in use and to find new keyword suggestions.

HOW does the Google Keyword Tool work?

Type in a word, phrase, or website name. The Google Keyword Tool will show you a list of similar keywords with a count of how often each word is searched. The competition column shows words that advertisers think have the most value.

WHO uses Keyword Tool?

(1) Website owners use the tool to test and find the best keywords to increase their website showing up on search engine pages.

(2) Advertisers with AdWords are main users of this tool, testing keywords to bid on for top ad placement on search pages.

(3) Sites earning Google income with Google AdSense use the tool to help focus page topics, and then select ad choices and ad locations for ads allowed on their website.

Newest Version: Google has offered different variations of this tool with different URL addresses including the old search-based Keyword Tool. Google recently combined all tools into one. This version replaces older versions. See also the Google Keyword Tool for Beginners and Keyword Video on Google's website.

✓ Save all	Search Terms (1)					
Keyword	Competition	Global Monthly Searches	Local Monthly Searches	Approximate CPC (Search)	Local Search Trends	
motor bike spares	Medium	4,400	2,400	£0.25		

✓ Save all	Keyword Ideas (800)					
Keyword	Competition	Global Monthly Searches	Local Monthly Searches	Approximate CPC (Search)	Local Search Trends	
bike spares	Medium	22,200	14,800	£0.28		
bike spares uk	High	4,400	2,900	£0.29		
motor bikes	Low	3,350,300	558,000	£0.37		
motorbike parts	Medium	368,000	90,500	£0.29		
motor bike shop	Medium	14,800	4,400	£0.40		
motorbike shops	Medium	673,500	135,000	£0.41		
pit bike spares	Medium	1,600	1,300	£0.26		
bike spare	High	22,200	5,400	£0.29		
motorcycle parts uk	Medium	9,900	6,600	£0.26		
suzuki bike spares uk	High	110	91	£0.24		
dirt bike spares	Medium	480	170	£0.28		
honda bike spares	High	880	480	£0.32		
suzuki parts uk	High	3,600	2,500	£0.28		
bike breakers uk	Medium	2,400	2,400	£0.21		
motorcycle spares uk	High	5,400	3,600	£0.25		
motorbike shop	Medium	823,000	135,000	£0.47		
bike spares ltd	Medium	170	110	£0.15		
motorbike parts online	High	12,100	1,000	£0.27		
honda bike parts	High	9,900	1,600	£0.30		
mini motors bikes	High	1,300	88	£0.31		
honda motor bikes	Low	450,300	27,100	£0.18		
classic motorcycle parts	Medium	4,500	1,900	£0.19		
quad bike spares	High	590	390	£0.24		
bike accessories uk	High	1,300	1,600	£0.40		

Okay, so the above looks like fairly heavy and comprehensive work; however, this should not deter you from starting your own web store or selling through Amazon or eBay as the keywords are vital. The real message is to keep it simple at the beginning and don't get too hung up on everything else, as this will only cause you to procrastinate.

How to get it right

Find the keywords that are required to drive your business forward. Use them in your domain name title, in your page headings, in paragraph headings where you may be bold or underlining the text, and especially ensure your keywords are part of your photographs and/or videos.

By using the free tools within Google you will be able to see how many people search for your keyword. You need to pay attention to the tick boxes on the side when you're entering your keyword into the Google analysis. You will have three to choose from:

1. Broad match. The default matching option, "broad match" means that your keyword may show if a search term contains your keyword terms in any order, and possibly along with other terms, singular or plural forms, synonyms, stemming (such as floor and flooring), related searches, and other relevant variations. Sticking with the broad match default is a great choice if you don't want to spend a lot of time building your keyword lists and want to capture the highest possible volume of ad traffic.

2. Exact match. Your keyword can appear when someone searches for your exact keyword, without any other terms in the search or when someone searches for close variants of that specific keyword. Close variants include misspellings, singular and plural forms, acronyms, stemming, abbreviations, and accents. The difference between "exact match" and "phrase match" (the next choice, below) is that if someone enters additional words before or after the keyword, your keyword won't show. Using exact match means that your keywords are targeted more precisely than broad match or phrase match. To use an exact match keyword, simply surround the words you want matched with brackets.

3. Phrase match. Your keyword can show when someone searches for your keyword with additional words before or after it. It will also show your keyword when someone searches for close variants of that exact keyword, or with additional words before or after it. Close variants include misspellings, singular and plural forms, acronyms, stemming, abbreviations, and accents. Using phrase match can help you reach more customers while still giving you more precise targeting. In other words, your keywords are less likely to show ads to customers searching for terms that aren't related to your product or service. To use a phrase match keyword, simply surround the words that you want matched with quotation marks.

There are other keyword sourcing tools out in the marketplace, and a particular favourite of mine is Market Samurai. You can download a free trial and then decide whether you want to use the paid version. I use the paid version as it gives me a lot more control over the information that I require and I can use the tools with more detail and accuracy than the free tools in Google.

Analyse your market

This is where I tend to use Market Samurai, as it gives me more functionality in drilling down to see what type of things people are searching for. I can also get the seasonality by month to ascertain when products are more likely to start selling or to start getting interest ready for sale in the next few weeks. It will also give me the information I need to see how much competition there is in the marketplace for my products as stated before. I believe it is key to ensure that I don't have a product that may have mass appeal but where profit and pricing is going to be continually driven down by hard competition from the big retailers with more buying power.

Google is always a good place to analyse your market by tapping in the product details and/or going onto some of the price comparison websites. You'll be able to get a feel for how high the competition level is for the product you're selling and whether the price points that you are creating are going to be sustainable in the marketplace. You also need to look at some of the big retailers to see what the price is now for your item, and then look to see what the price was during the particular time of the year.

As an example, consider toys. If you were to sell toys, then perhaps for nine months the price will be fairly sustainable with the profit margin being okay. However, consider the lead at Christmas, which of course is the busiest time for selling toys. At what point do the big retailers start discounting? Then you need to look at the size of the discounts they historically offer on the product line that you are potentially competing with them. If it's a line that they historically discount by up to 50% of the RRP then you need to check whether you can sustain such a low selling price during the peak selling period whilst still making a profit after you have paid any commission or fees.

Ask some questions

Another good way to get information is to do a survey. There are a number of ways of doing this. One way to is locally go face-to-face with people in the street, and it's always advisable to carry out your survey with complete strangers as they will tend to have no allegiance and no reason to tell you what they think you may want to hear, which is what friends and family often do because they will want to support you.

Here are some tips on how to write a survey. Your task is to write questions that each person who takes your survey will interpret in the same way. A good question should be short and straightforward. Do not use a long questionnaire; use plain English and do not make the questions difficult to answer. When putting your questionnaire together try to keep in mind the difference between what is *essential* to know against what's *useful* to know, and then discard any questions which will give you no useful information.

Write your questions so that everybody will understand them in the same way. Do not assume everyone has the same understanding of facts or has the same common knowledge. Always start your survey with the question that is interesting so that it will attract the respondent's attention. Take questions that might be difficult or threatening for later in the survey, and if you're using questions which are slightly difficult try using the third person approach, as this can be seen as less threatening. Always ensure you do not write leading questions, as they could demand a specific response that will lead to your questionnaire becoming a waste of time.

There are also some brilliant pieces of software that you can email to your mailing list. One that I and many of my acquaintances have used is www.surveymonkey.com. This type of survey sites allows you to put a survey together in a very short space of time so that you can collate the results coming back from the recipient. It also means it gives you an opportunity to possibly do some marketing within the survey, which may lead to additional sales.

Chapter 9: What You Know and Love Could Make Money Online

What do I know?

Many people come to me and say "I don't know anything," or "I can't sell anything as I have no knowledge of products I would want to sell" – the list is never-ending. However, here are a few tips. Get yourself a piece of paper, a pen, and sit somewhere quiet where you're not going to be interrupted for at least thirty minutes.

Start writing randomly the first thoughts that come into your head. At this point you don't need any order as you're not making a list, you're just randomly brain dumping onto the paper everything and anything that comes into your head. This is a brilliant exercise and you will end up after the first couple of minutes with several pages of information. You may have notes that you made cakes with your grandmother or that you washed cars at the weekend for pocket money, helping the allotment as a child. You may be a sports person and could start coaching other people. Note what jobs you had, what you were responsible for in those jobs, and what achievements, however small, you may have had in the workplace or in society through charitable activities. Write down your hobbies and your interests.

One of two things will happen when you're putting your list together. You may have a lightbulb moment when all of a sudden you know what you can do and what you're going to do; or you'll be able to take all that information and create a more detailed list which you can then look from an analytical perspective, adding more detail as you go along until you reach a point where you have enough information to make a decision.

What have I done in the past that may shape my future?

Very often it's what you've done in the past that you have written down on that piece of paper which will provide you with a clue. In my case it was quite simple– whilst at school I used to work for a wholesale fruit and vegetable merchant during the holidays, and upon leaving school I set up my first business buying and selling fruit and vegetables. I then got involved in a family business selling baby nursery goods both retail and wholesale along with running a small cafe. I then went to work for a very large national retailer and took on a customer service role that not only put me in front of customers but also gave me the opportunity to work with senior management on structuring customer service for that company. So you can see I'm now involved in internet retail, which is now the next stage on from high-street retail. So my past has shaped both my future and this business.

Do I have a passion, and is my passion enough?

Unless you're already a multimillionaire then you need to have energy, drive, ambition, and passion to take a business from zero to hero. If you're multimillionaire you can afford to employ people to do it for you, but for the purposes of this book I'm assuming that you're working in the business as well as working on the business.

Every business entrepreneur I have come across has a great passion and belief in what they do, and it is this that drives them forward so they can make a difference not just to their own life but also to the lives of the individuals they work with, employees, suppliers, and customers. There is a complete chain of events that gets unleashed when you start a business. It's like a drop of water falling into a still pond and you can watch the ripples spread out 360° from where the drop fell.

With a business that is up and running the one thing that all business owners and entrepreneurs should always do is invest in themselves. This may be through attending workshops, seminars, one-to-one training, or mentoring, because there are going to be times when you need to talk to somebody to find the answer to that question that is causing you a headache. Using mentors, coaches, and networking with other like-minded positive people are also keys to your success. Don't worry about proprietary information; nobody is going to pinch your wonderful idea because most of your fellow business people or entrepreneurs are too busy dealing with their own affairs to be thinking about stealing your ideas. So take advantage of telling other like-minded positive people what you're doing and you'll be surprised how much help and advice they will volunteer.

Chapter 10: The Seven Golden Rules to Guarantee Success

Your key strategy and your biggest challenge will be to deliver fantastic customer service. This means that sometimes you will have to accept that regardless of your legal position, your common sense, or just the plain fact that you know that what you have done is correct and the customer is not perhaps as honest as you would like them to be in that they are making false claims, customer challenges will happen and they will cost you money. You need to get over it and deliver the good customer service by taking the hit. Where a customer is wrong you do not have to serve them again, and if you're selling through eBay or Amazon and you have suspicions about this customer you can report them so the company can investigate. These instances will account for less than half of one per cent of your total business. When they do crop up, deal with them and then move on to something that will make you a profit.

1. Brilliant customer service

This starts even before the customer places the order. It's your feedback, it's your reviews, and it's your description of the product along with good photographs that start to build brilliant customer service. Where possible use a FAQ page (frequently asked questions) to deal with such enquiries as when do you normally ship, how do I pay, and what is your address for me to send you a postal order or cheque. Over a period of time you will build up a list of frequently asked questions; use that list to create your FAQ page.

When a customer sends you an email, reply to it as quickly as possible with a full response to the main body of the question. If as sometimes happens they ask you a question in a way that you do not understand what they require, reply with the information that you think covers their question leaving a suitable response to allow them to come back and clarify any further details. When you do respond to a question and you have placed the information in the listing, do not tell them to go back to the listing and look or sarcastically say to them "It's in the listing if you cared to look"; treat even than most silly questions as a real question. To your customer it's a real question and you do not know whether they are good at reading and interpreting information or whether they have some form of disability that requires them to seek further information than any other potential customer would.

Always list a telephone number, preferably a landline number that is not a premium rate call. If you can have difficulty servicing telephone calls then there are many agencies out there that will redirect your call and provide an answering messages service for you. The services do attract cost although they can be extremely reasonable if it means that you plan your day to return calls between 4pm and 6pm. These messaging services can take a lot of the information and detail the customer requires so that when you get the notification you may be able to answer the question in full. However, if you're going to use an answering machine ensure that this has an adequate outgoing message that states an approximate time frame that you will look to return calls and/or deal with any questions. A professional message on your answering machine will encourage a potential caller to leave a message. However, if you are taking payments by telephone there is a great chance that you will lose sales by not having the telephone answered correctly.

My experience is that with the right person answering the telephone in a professional manner and dealing with the call immediately as it should be we can convert more questions into sales. We can also convert more complaints into very positive customer feedback and solutions that work for both of us. It's interesting that once I have had my customer service team dealing with an issue, the customer has either been very grateful in their praise of the customer service agent and/or they have purchased further items from us due to the good customer service they received.

Top Tip: Rule number one is that the customer is always right. Rule number two is that if ever the customer is wrong, re-read the rule number one.

2. Over deliver and under promise

One way I get massive and exceptional feedback is by ensuring that the customer's expectations are managed to a point that they think my team is totally excellent, which of course they are. Here is just a very small sample of some of the comments left on one of my eBay shops:

- Really quick delivery, thanks!!
- Excellent
- Really pleased, lovely item, quick dispatch and thanks for free P&P
- Great for my friends hen night many giggles. Thank you!
- Deffo use again thanks
- Quick delivery
- beautiful cat! Thank you!
- Friendly,Helpful,Great seller.Superfast Shipping Thank you. Take care AAAAA+++
- Top seller

And here's a small selection from one of our Amazon sites.

Rating	Comments	Arrived on Time	Item as Described	Customer Service
5	delivery excellent article excellent what more can be said RESPOND	Yes	Yes	Yes
5	all as decribed RESPOND	Yes	Yes	Yes
5	Great seller very helpful thank you RESPOND	Yes	Yes	Yes
5	Great service RESPOND	Yes	Yes	Yes
5	Perfect - as described RESPOND	Yes	Yes	Yes
5	my little girl absolutely loves this. great product. RESPOND	Yes	Yes	Yes
5	Good product RESPOND	Yes	Yes	Yes
5	Look good and are as described. RESPOND	Yes	Yes	-
5	Very fast delivery RESPOND	-	-	-
5	Great service RESPOND	Yes	Yes	Yes
5	Really pleased with this, quick delivery. Thanks RESPOND	Yes	Yes	-

Isn't it wonderful to get such great and positive feedback? It makes you realise that you're doing a good job and you have something that the customer wants. But when a customer looks at it, their expectations are very high so you cannot afford to let the good work slip by falling into sloppy habits.

Top Tip: You're only as good as your last piece of feedback.

3. Stay in touch

Communication, communication, communication. Talk to your customer, make them feel valuable, and let them believe that they are the most important person in the world. They see themselves as most important people in the world and they need to feel valued.

When you're sending them a parcel you're going to put a thank you note in their package with all your contact details and a very special offer to existing customers only. Are you going to invite them to be an exclusive member of your mailing list for any special offers or valuable information that will be of value to them? You have their address, phone number, and email address, and with brilliant systems you can approach your customers on a regular basis with repeat offers.

You need to be aware that there are protocols for contacting people and we strongly suggest that you get their agreement to contact them on a regular basis. By doing this and not mass-market into them you will be saving money and be focusing on customers who want to hear from you and have a higher potential of purchasing from you again because they have come to know you and trust your customer service.

There are many ways of setting up marketing campaigns by using email broadcasts, text messaging, mailshots, telephone marketing, and newsletters, or if the value of the repeat business is potentially big enough you can always send them a free gift. You will get people that will ask you to remove them from your mailing list and you need to respect this request and do what they ask. There is nothing to stop you going back to them and asking them the reason they wish to be removed from the list; however, if you do this be very tactful in your response in order that you will get a positive or polite reply back.

4. Fix the problem – Do not procrastinate

It's very common for small businesses to protect their position and not necessarily fix the problem. Do not procrastinate when a problem arises. Go out of your way to fix it quickly, and show the customer that you have a sense of urgency in dealing with the matter. If you do need to have an investigation into the background of the problem, do it once it has been dealt with. Do not use various tactics that I come across, such as saying, "We need to talk to the manufacturer" or "I need to speak to…." You do not need to do any of these things; you need to fix the problem with speed. Once it's fixed, of course you can then get on with selling more products or services to make more profit.

There is a caveat to this. If you have a customer that is not playing by the rules and their problem is not genuine, then you may need to go down the route of an investigation. Where this is the case you should follow the same guidelines and not procrastinate. If you need to have the item back and assess it for repair replacement under warranty do this with speed and ensure the customer is fully aware of the process and the timing that the process may take. This way you're managing this customer's expectations. Let's say that you normally would take five days to assess and report on the problem. In your customer service manual allow seven days and then deliver your findings in four days. In this way you have managed your customer's expectations and have over delivered by providing the information in a shorter period of time.

When you have to go down this route try not to be overbearing or come across as aggressive in stating the details of your terms and conditions of sale and/or warranty. Stay reasonable at all times and look at this opportunity as being one to convert a customer with a problem into a raving fan for your business who will tell other people in their circle how great you were at dealing with the issue that they had.

5. Make sure you would accept your own customer service

Take a look at your terms and conditions that your business presently operates in, and with a fresh cup of coffee and an open mind go through your customer service procedures as if you were a customer on the receiving end of them. Would you be happy with your customer service?

If you have a large business and can test your customer service, purchase your own product and then contact your service department by telephone and/or email with a fictitious problem. You'll be able to find some historical common problems and replicate them to see the end result. If required, ask a friend who is not known by your company to make the purchase and use their contact details to test the customer service that you are giving. I'm always amazed by the number of fairly large companies that never telephone their own offices to find out how potential customers are treated by the sales team, customer service representatives or even the receptionist. Do you know how your customers are treated when they call in?

Employ the services of a mystery shopper. Give them an exact brief on the information they should be able to obtain from your staff. They don't necessarily need to make a purchase, but they should be able to go through the process you have in place up to the point of making a purchase. I have used this many times so that I can ascertain how my staff behaves towards my customers; and yes, I have let staff go when I have found out what happens when I'm not immediately available and I have left people in charge. Remember this is your business and you need to have checks and balances in place to ensure that you're delivering the best customer service – and your team plays a crucial role in ensuring this happens.

6. Manage your feedback website comments

If you're using your own web shop then it's vital that you obtain customer feedback. The best way to do this is to allow comments to be posted directly to your website, but ensure that all comments have to be viewed and/or edited by you before they go on the website as you need to maintain and retain control over those comments. Anybody that comes to you with a negative comment, deal with it and resolve it to the best of your ability and to the customer's satisfaction so that they will in turn give you back some positive feedback. Then of course they can leave positive comments on your website.

As a word of caution I would urge you not to falsify any comments or reviews to your website. Not only is this misleading but it also calls into question your own personal integrity and the integrity of your business. You need to be dealing with your customers from a point of view of openness and fairness where your honesty and integrity can never be questioned.

7. Honest descriptions and good photographs

As you will gather from my previous comments customer service is key to having a business that works and that you can repeat sell time and time again. Two of the areas that you must pay very particular attention to are your descriptions and your photographs. I see on a regular basis many items for sale with such a poor description that I do not know what I'm buying. People do not put time dimensions, they may not say whether it's new or used, if it's a limited edition, how much does it weigh, what are its features and how do they benefit me. I get lots of feedback from my customers with the words "as described," which tells me that the time I have taken to ensure the description is accurate has been well worth it.

When you're describing a product you must ensure that your description is full and accurate. Do not rely on the manufacturer's web page or other people's descriptions that you just copy and paste. Do not do this as you are leaving yourself wide open to having negative feedback along with poor customer service ratings. Take the time to ensure your description is complete, accurate, has colour choice, and where there is a variation or choice of designs, styles, or sizes, include the details regarding the variation. A very good way to ensure that your description is readable and understandable is to ask a friend or colleague to proofread it and make any very honest comments about how they understand or perceive it.

Always include in any description the size of the product, the weight of the product, and any relevant information regarding the packaging and shipping of the product so the customer can fully understand what they are purchasing.

Here is a listing that shows you what you must *not* do that I found very quickly on eBay:

mirror

Description   Postage and payments

Seller assumes all responsibility for this listing

Item specifics

Condition   Used. An item that has been previously used. The item may have some signs of cosmetic wear.

Large wooded surround mirror

As you can see from this particular listing the item is described as "Mirror." There are no dimensions, there are no details about the condition other than it was in the used category, no manufacturer, just no information whatsoever, except for free delivery. I'm not able to include the photograph as it actually contained a full view of the person taking the photograph!

Top Tip: Use a little reverse engineering when listing items. Have a look at any competitors who are selling the same or similar items, and review their descriptions. Take the best points that capture your focus and adapt those to the items you are listing. Always look at a listing from the point of view of what you would want to read about the item in both its description along with its technical detail. Always keep it simple and well structured.

Bonus Page

You're now at the beginning of what can be one of the most lucrative and rewarding opportunities to make a difference to your wealth – both your financial wealth and your spiritual wealth. It's a good idea now to celebrate how far you have come with the new knowledge that you have gained whilst looking for more new knowledge to help you achieve your goals.

As part of the range of books now available there are also opportunities to meet the author by attending workshops where you can have a one-to-one discussion about your business, plans, and opportunities.

I have provided five FREE bonuses, and these can be downloaded from the website www.h2so.org/free-stuff

The five bonuses are:

We will send them or the details of how to register directly to your inbox the following:

FREE Top 10 Amazon Mistakes And How To Avoid Them

FREE Chapter Of The Book On How To Sell On EBay

FREE 20 Minute Invitation For A Telephone Consultation With The Author Andrew Whitfield

One Half-Price Workshop Of Your Choice

The Opportunity To Take Advantage Six Months FREE Membership To How To Sell Online When Purchasing An Annual Membership Package

Once again I would like to thank you for purchasing my book and if you ever need to contact me or my team just go to our main website www.h2so.org

www.ingramcontent.com/pod-product-compliance
Lightning Source LLC
Chambersburg PA
CBHW051716170526
45167CB00002B/688